D1550717

Memorial Day

By Karen Latchana Kenney
Illustrated by Judith A. Hunt

Content Consultant:
Richard Jensen, PhD
Author, Scholar, and Historian

magic
wagon

visit us at www.abdopublishing.com

Published by Magic Wagon, a division of the ABDO Group, 8000 West 78th Street, Edina, Minnesota, 55439. Copyright © 2011 by Abdo Consulting Group, Inc. International copyrights reserved in all countries. All rights reserved. No part of this book may be reproduced in any form without written permission from the publisher.

Looking Glass Library™ is a trademark and logo of Magic Wagon.

Printed in the United States of America, North Mankato, Minnesota.
092010
012011
 THIS BOOK CONTAINS AT LEAST 10% RECYCLED MATERIALS.

Text by Karen Latchana Kenney
Illustrations by Judith A. Hunt
Edited by Melissa Johnson
Interior layout and design by Becky Daum
Cover design by Becky Daum

Library of Congress Cataloging-in-Publication Data
Kenney, Karen Latchana.
 Memorial Day / by Karen Latchana Kenney ; illustrated by Judith A. Hunt.
    p. cm. — (Our nation's pride)
 Includes index.
 ISBN 978-1-61641-152-7
 1. Memorial Day—Juvenile literature. I. Hunt, Judith A., 1955- ill. II. Title.
 E642.K34 2011
 394.262—dc22
                            2010013998

Table of Contents

Remembering a Soldier

People walk slowly among the rows of a cemetery. Here, beneath white grave markers, soldiers are buried. At one grave, a woman lays flowers on the grass. She remembers her grandfather. He fought in a war long ago.

It is the last Monday in May. The people have come to observe Memorial Day. This day honors U.S. soldiers who have died while serving in the military.

4

The Civil War

Memorial Day has its roots in the American Civil War. From 1861 to 1865, the United States was divided. The states in the North fought the states in the South. The South wanted to be a separate country.

The two sides fought many battles that ended in bloodshed. More than 620,000 soldiers died. Many families lost a son, a brother, or a father. After four years of fighting, the nation remained united.

Decoration Day

People wanted to honor the dead soldiers after the war. They put flowers and flags on the soldiers' graves. People in different towns did this on different days.

In 1868, a group of soldiers announced May 30 would be a special day. It was called Decoration Day. Now, everyone in the nation remembered the American Civil War soldiers on the same day.

A Service at Arlington

On the first Decoration Day, people gathered at Arlington National Cemetery. This is a military cemetery in Arlington, Virginia. Many soldiers from the American Civil War are buried here.

A crowd of 5,000 people listened as famous army generals spoke. Visitors placed small flags and flowers on the graves.

A Changing Holiday

In 1914, World War I broke out. The countries of Europe fought each other. The United States entered the war in 1917. Many U.S. soldiers died in the war.

In 1918, the war ended, and Decoration Day changed. Now, it would honor soldiers who died in all wars, not just the American Civil War. People started calling the holiday Memorial Day.

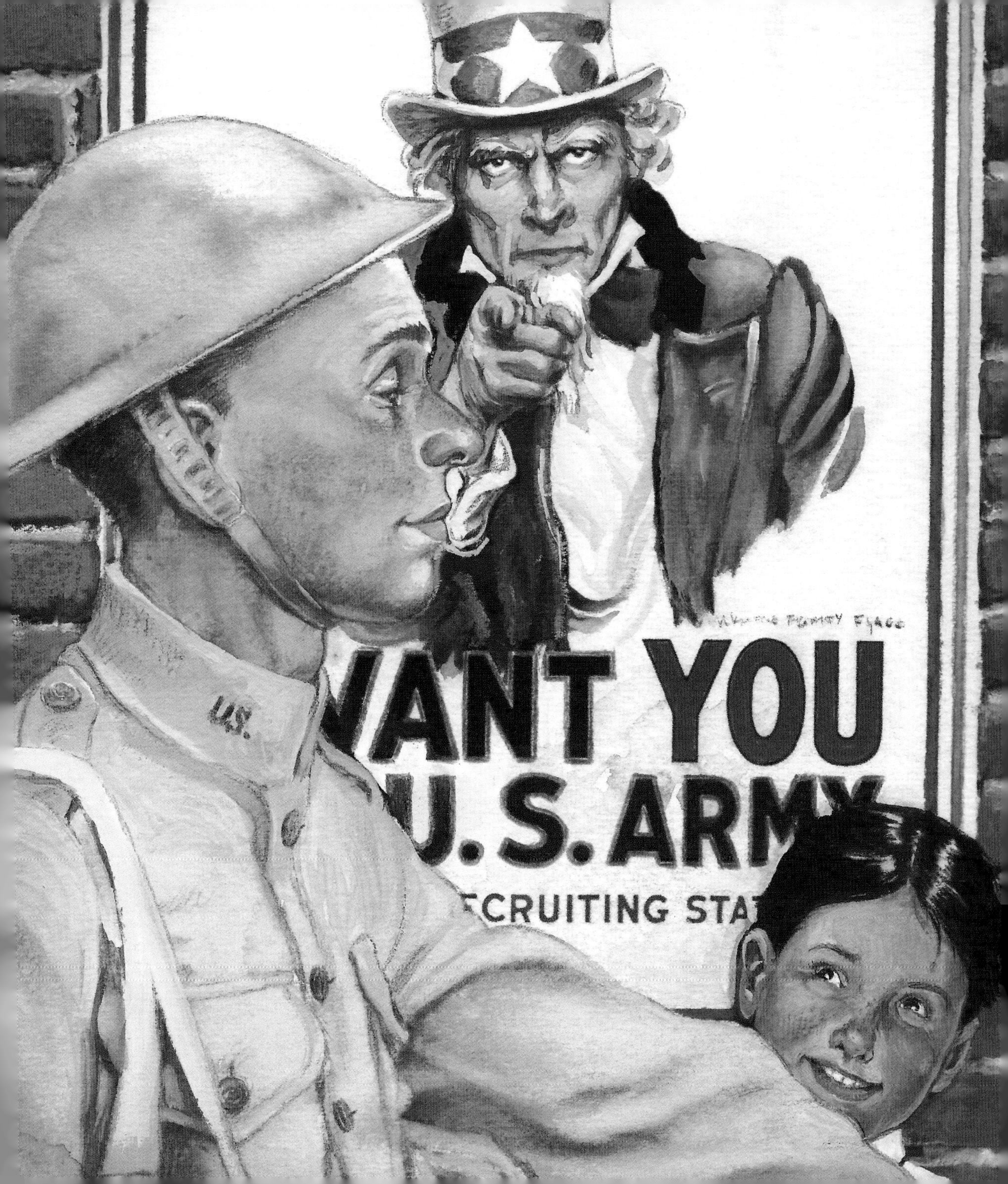

VANT YOU
U.S. ARMY
ECRUITING STA
U.S.

A National Holiday

Over time, each state passed laws to make May 30 an official state holiday. In 1971, a law made Memorial Day a national holiday.

As a national holiday, many things about Memorial Day changed. Now, the holiday is on the last Monday in May. On that Monday, schools and the government shut down. Many people have the day off to remember the nation's fallen soldiers.

The Flag on
Memorial Day

On Memorial Day, U.S. flags on government buildings start the day at half-mast. They fly in the middle of the flagpoles. This shows respect for military people who have died in wars. At noon, the flags are raised again to the tops of the poles.

Flags In

A special service called *Flags In* starts on the Friday before Memorial Day. Flags In takes place at two military cemeteries. They are Arlington National Cemetery and the U.S. Soldiers' and Airmen's Home National Cemetery.

During Flags In, soldiers walk through the cemeteries. They put small flags on each grave. The soldiers make sure the flags stay on the graves until Memorial Day.

A Moment to Remember

In December 2000, a new law created the National Moment of Remembrance. This is a new way to honor people who have died in war.

On 3:00 p.m. on Memorial Day, people stop what they are doing. They stay silent for one minute. They remember soldiers who have died.

"Taps"

During the moment of silence, a military person may play "Taps" on a bugle. This instrument is like a trumpet. The beautiful song has a simple, haunting melody. It is also played at military funerals.

Red Poppies

A poppy is another symbol for Memorial Day. A famous war poem was written about the red flowers. Now, they remind people of those who have died in wars.

Soldiers' groups pay sick or injured veterans to make poppies all year. On Memorial Day, they give the flowers away. People give money to the groups to help the veterans. They wear poppies to show that soldiers are not forgotten.

24

Observing Memorial Day

Parades are another important part of Memorial Day. Towns close down streets. People line up along the sidewalks. Veterans and military people march through the crowds to the beat of a marching band.

There are so many ways to pay respect on

Memorial Day. The next final Monday in May,

remember the people in the military who have

died. Thank them for protecting your country.

Fun Facts

- At first, many states in the South did not celebrate Decoration Day after the Civil War. They continued to choose separate days to honor the soldiers of the South.

- People in different towns believe Memorial Day started in their town. On May 26, 1966, Waterloo, New York, became the "Birthplace of Memorial Day."

- U.S. presidents visit Arlington National Cemetery in Virginia on Memorial Day. They put wreaths on the Tomb of the Unknown Soldier. This is a memorial to all of the soldiers who could not be identified after their deaths.

- A big concert is held on the lawn of the U.S. Capitol on the day before Memorial Day. It is called the National Memorial Day Concert.

Glossary

cemetery—a place where many people are buried.

funeral—a service for someone who has died.

grave—the spot where a person is buried in a cemetery.

memorial—something that is made to remember a person or an event.

military—the armed forces that protect a country. The five branches of the U.S. military are Air Force, Army, Coast Guard, Navy, and Marines.

symbol—something that stands for something else.

veteran—a person who has served in the military.

On the Web

To learn more about Memorial Day, visit ABDO Group online at **www.abdopublishing.com**. Web sites about Memorial Day are featured on our Book Links page. These links are routinely monitored and updated to provide the most current information available.

Index